Professor Wormbog's Gloomy Kerploppus

A Book of Great Smells
(and a heart-warming story, besides)

BY MERCER MAYER

gb Golden Press • New York
Western Publishing Company, Inc.
Racine, Wisconsin

 NE day, Professor Wormbog's pet Kerploppus was very gloomy. He wouldn't eat his bowl of grapes or play fetch the stick. He just lay in his bed and sighed all day.

"Oh dear," thought the professor. "I had better call Doctor Windbag. Surely he will know what to do. After all, he is a doctor."

Doctor Windbag was just fixing himself a
cucumber sandwich when the professor called. He
put the sandwich in his hat and rushed right over.

"Oh, my, yes," said the doctor. "Your Kerploppus certainly does look gloomy. The best thing to do is bathe him in fresh cucumber juice. Call me if he doesn't seem better."

Professor Wormbog picked bushels and bushels
of cucumbers from his garden.

He boiled up a big pot of them
and bathed his Kerploppus in the juice
all night long.

In the morning, the Kerploppus
still wouldn't eat his breakfast or fetch
his stick.

ALL NIGHT!

I'm afraid
of spiders.

HEY, SCRATCH
AND SNIFF THESE
CUCUMBERS.
WOW! TOO MUCH!

"Doctor Windbag," complained Professor Wormbog, "my Kerploppus is still very gloomy."

"Well, well," answered the doctor, who was just about to mow the yard. "Take the little fella on a picnic in the country. That will surely cheer him up."

Off they went to the country, with the Kerploppus all
bundled up so he wouldn't catch a chill. The grass was
green, and all the flowers were in bloom, but the Kerploppus
didn't cheer up.

He just sat around
and sighed all day.

On the way home, they even stopped for burgers and shakes, but it didn't help a bit.

"This room is very gloomy," said Doctor Windbag. "Why don't you paint it with bright, cheery colors? That will surely make him feel better."

Professor Wormbog got some bright, cheery paint from the cellar.

He painted the room, but it did no good. Besides, the fresh paint made the Kerploppus sneeze.

To pass the time while the paint dried,
they took a steamship cruise to the South Pacific.

They sipped coconut juice and dined on fresh bananas and pineapples. They danced the hula under the swaying palm trees, but the Kerploppus didn't care.

Professor Wormbog called Doctor Windbag long-distance. "I'm worried," he said.

"Come home at once," replied the doctor.

"We must kick this problem around."

They hurried home and Professor Wormbog rushed his Kerploppus to Doctor Windbag's office.

"I shall take an X ray," announced the doctor. He turned on the X-ray machine. "My goodness!" he exclaimed. "What can this be?"

Grabbing the Kerploppus by the feet, he shook him upside down. Out fell a big boot.

"Hmmm," said Professor Wormbog. "I was wondering where my other boot went."

Doctor Windbag gave them a great big bag of peppermint candy canes for being so good. Then Professor Wormbog took his Kerploppus home.

HEY KIDS, SCRATCH AND SNIFF THE CANDY CANES DOCTOR WINDBAG GAVE US.
LET'S EAT 'EM ALL BEFORE DINNER.

That night, they had a wonderful feast with all the
good things the Kerploppus loved. He ate everything.